HEALTHY FOOD
CHOICES

Dinner

Vic Parker

Heinemann
LIBRARY
Chicago, Illinois

To contact Capstone Global Library, please call
800-747-4992, or visit our web site
www.capstonepub.com

Edited by Rebecca Rissman, Dan Nunn, and
    Diyan Leake
Designed by Philippa Jenkins
Original illustrations © Capstone Global
    Library Ltd 2014
Picture research by Tracy Cummins
Production by Helen McCreath
Originated by Capstone Global Library Ltd
Printed and bound in China

17 16 15 14 13
10 9 8 7 6 5 4 3 2 1

Library of Congress Cataloging-in-Publication Data
Parker, Victoria, author.
  Dinner / Vic Parker.
      pages cm.—(Healthy food choices)
  Summary: "Read Dinner to learn how to make healthy
food choices during this evening meal. Different photos
show healthy and unhealthy dinner options, while simple
text explains why some choices are better than others.
A dinner foods quiz concludes the book."—Provided by
publisher.
  Includes bibliographical references and index.
  ISBN 978-1-4329-9118-0 (hb)—ISBN 978-1-4329-
9123-4 (pb) 1. Nutrition—Juvenile literature. 2.
Dinners and dining—Juvenile literature. 3. Health—
Juvenile literature. I. Title.
  TX355.P2545 2014
  613.2—dc23   2013015691

Acknowledgments
We would like to thank the following for permission
to reproduce photographs: Capstone Publishers
(Karon Dubke) pp. 4, 7, 8, 9, 10, 11, 12, 13, 14,
15, 16, 17, 18, 19, 20, 21, 22, 23, 24, 25, 26, 27;
ChooseMyPlate.gov p. 29 (with thanks to USDA's Center
for Nutrition Policy and Promotion); Getty Images pp. 5
(Karl Weatherly), 6 (Fuse).

Cover photograph of roasted salmon with penne and
broccoli reproduced with permission of Getty Images
(Joseph De Leo) and fish and French fries reproduced
with permision of Shutterstock (© Joe Gough).

Every effort has been made to contact copyright
holders of material reproduced in this book. Any
omissions will be rectified in subsequent printings if
notice is given to the publisher.

All the Internet addresses (URLs) given in this book were
valid at the time of going to press. However, due to the
dynamic nature of the Internet, some addresses may
have changed, or sites may have changed or ceased to
exist since publication. While the author and publisher
regret any inconvenience this may cause readers, no
responsibility for any such changes can be accepted by
either the author or the publisher.

Contents

 Some words are shown in bold, **like this.** You can find out what they mean by looking in the glossary.

Why Make Healthy Choices?

We cannot live for long without food and water. To be healthy, your body needs different kinds of foods, in the right amounts for your age and size. You also need at least six glasses of water every day.

Your brain and body need food and water to be able to think, move, grow, and repair any injuries.

Eating healthy foods helps us to enjoy life.

If you eat healthy food, you will feel and look healthy. If you eat unhealthy food, you will feel and look unhealthy. You may become too thin or **overweight**. You may lack energy and feel tired and grumpy. You may even become sick.

What Makes a Dinner Healthy or Unhealthy?

Eating a healthy dinner will fill you up and help you sleep well at night. But some dinners are healthier than others. For instance, a hot dog dinner can be high in **saturated fat,** which can clog up your heart and blood vessels.

Dinner is the perfect opportunity for your family to spend time together.

To stay healthy, you need to eat the right number of calories for your age, your size, and the amount of exercise you get.

fried hamburgers, creamy mashed potatoes, buttered peas, gravy
800 calories

grilled hamburgers, steamed potatoes, and peas
545 calories

Food gives you energy, which is measured in **calories.** Foods can be high or low in calories, depending on what they are and how they are cooked. Eating too many calories at meal and snack times can make you **overweight.** Eating too few can make you too thin.

Meat

Meat is an excellent source of **protein**. Your body needs protein to grow and to repair skin and muscle. However, **red meat**, such as a steak, can be high in fat, especially if it is fried. Eating it with French fries can make your dinner even higher in unhealthy **saturated fat** and **calories**.

Red meat is usually much higher in fat than white meat such as chicken.

fried mushrooms

fried fatty steak

fries

When you can choose, ask for **lean** cuts of red meat rather than fatty cuts.

grilled mushrooms

oven-baked sweet potato wedges with skin on

grilled lean steak

Grilling red meat is healthier than frying it, since it does not add fat. You can also grill mushrooms instead of frying them. Choose sweet potato wedges baked with their skin on, rather than French fries. These are low in fat and high in **fiber**, which keeps your **digestive system** working properly.

Pizza

Store-bought pizzas are **processed** foods that contain **artificial additives** such as **preservatives, flavoring,** and **coloring.** Artificial additives can be unhealthy and even harmful. White-flour dough has little **fiber** and few **vitamins** or **minerals.** Cheese and processed meat are high in **saturated fat** and **sodium.**

processed tomato sauce

white-flour dough

three types of cheese

processed meat

cheese-stuffed crust

Half a large stuffed-crust pepperoni pizza contains more **calories** than an eight-year-old needs in a day.

Healthy pizzas are fun to make at home. Prepare a **whole wheat** dough for lots of fiber and long-lasting energy. For toppings that are full of **nutrients** but low in fat, sodium, and artificial additives, use low-fat cheese, fresh vegetables, and fish.

steamed green vegetables

thin whole wheat crust

low-fat cheese

Pizza can be high in calories, so eat a moderate amount and fill up on healthy salad.

salad

homemade fresh tomato sauce

Pasta

Pasta is full of **carbohydrates,** which give you energy. However, some pasta dinners are much healthier than others. Macaroni and cheese is high in **saturated fat, sodium,** and **calories** and low in **fiber, vitamins,** and **minerals.**

Macaroni and cheese can be an occasional treat, but it is not healthy as an everyday dinner.

cheesy sauce

white-flour pasta

whole wheat pasta

Whole wheat pasta is healthy and filling.

onions

tomatoes

zucchinis

red peppers

yellow peppers

Whole wheat pasta is a good source of healthy fiber. It also releases energy slowly, so it keeps you going for longer. A pasta sauce made of fresh tomatoes and other vegetables is full of vitamins, minerals, and **antioxidants** that fight disease.

Rice

Rice forms the basis of many dinners. It is a good source of energy and it is low in **saturated fat.** However, it is often eaten in unhealthy ways. For instance, egg fried rice served with sweet and sour pork is high in saturated fat and sugar.

Frying foods adds saturated fat and **calories**.

sugary sweet and sour sauce

deep-fried battered balls of pork

egg fried white rice

Brown rice is even healthier than white rice. This is because it contains seven times as much **fiber**. With a serving of **tofu**, fresh vegetables, and raw nuts, brown rice makes a low-fat meal full of **vitamins**, **minerals**, **protein**, and long-lasting energy.

raw peanuts

tofu

broccoli

yellow pepper

red pepper

brown rice

A stir-fry uses very little vegetable oil, so it is a healthy way of cooking.

Fish

Fish is a healthy choice for dinner. It is low in fat but packed with **protein, vitamins,** and **minerals.** Fish has healthy fats that protect the heart. However, certain recipes turn fish into an unhealthy dinner. Frying fish and eating it with French fries turns it into a meal high in **saturated fat** and **calories.**

fried fish

fries

This meal has lots of calories.

It is good to eat fish at least twice a week. Make sure it is cooked in a healthy way.

boiled brown rice

grilled fish fillet

salad

Choosing an unbattered fillet of fish will give you all of its **nutrients** without adding anything unhealthy. Grilling is a healthy, low-fat way to cook the fish. Boiled rice is much lower in fat than French fries. Fresh salad adds vitamins and minerals.

Burritos and Wraps

A tortilla is a round flatbread that can be filled and rolled up to make many kinds of dishes. A burrito is made of a flour tortilla often filled with beef, refried beans, cheese, and sour cream. This is a high-**saturated-fat**, high-**calorie** dinner.

white-flour tortilla

sour cream

beef

refried beans

cheddar cheese

A large-sized burrito with fatty fillings is an unhealthy food.

whole wheat tortilla

homemade guacamole

turkey breast

Eat a moderate-sized burrito or wrap, so it is not too high in calories. Fill up on healthy salad.

lettuce

tomato

cucumber

kidney beans

sunflower seeds

Swap some ingredients to make a burrito or wrap much more healthy. Use a **whole wheat** tortilla for more **fiber** and longer-lasting energy. Choose a low-fat meat such as turkey instead of beef. Canned kidney beans, low-fat cheese, and homemade guacamole are low-calorie fillings.

Grilling

Grilling food outside can be a fun way to cook dinner when the weather is hot. However, coating fatty meat in sugary barbecue sauce before it is grilled is not healthy. Salads with creamy dressing and buttered white rolls add more **saturated fat,** with little **fiber, vitamins,** or **minerals.**

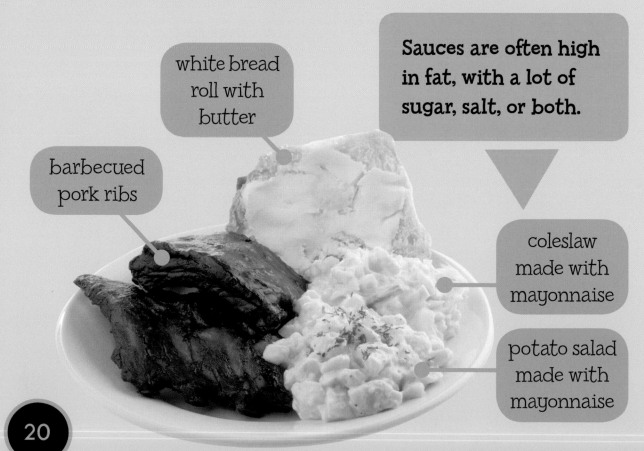

white bread roll with butter

Sauces are often high in fat, with a lot of sugar, salt, or both.

barbecued pork ribs

coleslaw made with mayonnaise

potato salad made with mayonnaise

Grilling food outdoors can be a healthy way to cook.

whole grain roll

coleslaw made with low-fat yogurt

onion

fish

tomato

red pepper

A much healthier way to grill is to choose fish or white meat such as chicken. Avoid coating them in dressings. Threading chunks on skewers with pieces of vegetable makes a colorful meal full of **protein**, vitamins, and minerals. Toss salads in a little low-fat yogurt and choose **whole grain** rolls with low-fat spread.

Desserts

A dessert can be a tasty way to end dinner. However, some desserts, such as store-bought cakes, can be high in **saturated fat** and **sodium**. Other desserts, such as strawberry pie and ice cream, can be high in saturated fat and sugar.

Many desserts are unhealthy.

whipped cream

ice cream

high-fat crust

sugary, high-**calorie** filling

frozen low-fat
yogurt

strawberries

Healthy dessert
choices can be
delicious.

Fresh fruit with frozen yogurt is a healthy, tasty dessert. You could also try stirring chopped fresh fruit into a tub of low-fat yogurt. These desserts are low in saturated fat and filled with **fiber, vitamins,** and **minerals.**

Drinks

Many people like to drink sugary soda with their dinner. Some have a milk-based drink such as a milkshake or hot cocoa at bedtime. Soda is high in sugar. Diet drinks are not much healthier. They are high in **artificial sweetener,** which can be harmful in large amounts. Drinks made with whole milk can be high in **saturated fat.**

soda

cocoa

Whole milk and store-bought juices can be very high in **calories.**

milkshake

Drinks made with low-fat or nonfat milk are much healthier than whole milk drinks. They are lower in saturated fat, but still high in **calcium**. Your body needs calcium to build strong bones and teeth. Water is a very healthy choice of drink. Every part of your body needs water to work properly.

water

low-fat milk

Choose a healthy drink to go with your healthy dinner.

Food Quiz

Take a look at these roasted chicken dinners. Can you figure out which picture shows an unhealthy dinner and which shows a healthier dinner, and why?

roasted chicken, skin on

store-bought gravy

roasted potatoes

cheesy cauliflower

honey-glazed baked carrots

boiled potatoes

roasted chicken
without skin

homemade gravy

steamed
cauliflower

boiled carrots

The answer is on the next page.

Food Quiz Answers

This is the unhealthy dinner. While there is chicken for **protein**, potatoes for energy, and vegetables for **vitamins** and **minerals**, the cooking methods mean that there is also a lot of **saturated fat** and sugar. Store-bought gravy often contains a lot of **sodium** as well as fat.

This is the healthy dinner. The roasted chicken without the skin is a good source of protein that is lower in fat. Boiling and steaming the vegetables means that no sugar or fat is added. Homemade gravy is much lower in sodium than store-bought kinds. Did you guess correctly?

Tips for Healthy Eating

Use this MyPlate guide to choose the right amounts of different foods for good health. Choose low-fat cooking methods and do not add salt (it is high in **sodium**). Don't forget to drink several glasses of water and to exercise every day.

ChooseMyPlate.gov

See if you can get the right balance over the course of a whole day.

Glossary

antioxidant substance that helps your body fight off disease

artificial additive human-made substance that is added to food, such as coloring, flavoring, and preservatives

artificial sweetener human-made substance that can be added to food to give it a sweet taste

calcium mineral your body needs to build strong bones and teeth. Calcium is found in dairy foods and in some vegetables, nuts, and seeds.

calorie unit we use for measuring energy

carbohydrate substance in starchy foods (such as potatoes, pasta, and rice) and sugary foods that gives you energy

coloring something added to food to make it look attractive

digestive system all the body parts that break down food so the body can use it

fiber part of certain plants that passes through your body without being broken down. This helps other foods to pass through your stomach, too.

flavoring something added to food to make it taste better

lean describes meat that has little fat or that has had the fatty parts trimmed off

mineral natural substance, such as iron, that is essential for health

nutrient substance in food that is good for your body, such as vitamins, minerals, and antioxidants

overweight heavier than is healthy for your age and height

preservative something added to food to make it last longer

processed made or prepared in a factory. Processed foods often contain artificial additives.

protein natural substance that your body needs to build skin, muscle, and other tissues. Protein is found in foods such as meat, fish, and beans.

red meat meat, such as beef, lamb, and pork, that is red when raw

saturated fat type of fat found in butter, fatty cuts of meat, cheese, and cream. It is bad for your heart.

sodium natural substance found in salt

tofu food made from bean curd. It is high in protein and calcium and low in fat and calories.

vitamin natural substance that is essential for good health

whole grain made with every part of the grain, without removing any of the inner or outer parts

whole wheat made with wheat flour that uses every part of the grain, without removing any of the inner or outer parts

Find Out More

Books

Graimes, Nicola, and Howard Shooter. *Kids' Fun and Healthy Cookbook*. New York: Dorling Kindersley, 2007.

Parker, Vic. *All About Meat and Fish* (Food Zone). Irvine, Calif.: QEB, 2009.

Parker, Vic. *All About Vegetables* (Food Zone). Irvine, Calif.: QEB, 2009.

Internet sites

Facthound offers a safe, fun way to find Internet sites related to this book. All of the sites on Facthound have been researched by our staff.

Here's all you do:
Visit **www.facthound.com**
Type in this code: 9781432991180

Index